CW01064859

DANCING THROUGH DOORWAYS

DANCING THROUGH DOORWAYS

Siân Thornthwaite

The Book Guild Ltd
Sussex, England

First published in Great Britain in 2000 by
The Book Guild Ltd
25 High Street
Lewes, East Sussex
BN7 2LU

Typesetting in Bembo by
IML Typographers, Chester, Cheshire

Printed in Great Britain by
Bookcraft (Bath) Ltd

A catalogue record for this book is available from
The British Library.

ISBN 1 85776 571 0

CONTENTS

Berlin – 1984

The wall it divides, cuts and it scars
A perfect city, its delight how it mars
The modern and brash, the old and the new
Even the pretty, the borrowed and blue
East and West married by men of the world
Politicians they made it – Berlin unfurled
The curtain arose on divided dreams
A political nightmare is all it now seems
Graves at the Reichstag enlighten the plight
The seemingly perfect yet endless fight
Against oppression, freedom so dear
The East is in torment, so far, yet so near
Allowed to view, yet a lifetime away
Kept at a distance – and that way to stay?
The façade, a city of beauty and charm
The reality, the tension never calm
Two nations unite, and give the precious gift
Break up the wall, destroy the great rift
Stop this chess with Berliner as pawn
And start today, a new political dawn

Ph. D. Blues

The start of a dream – a Ph. D. place
If only I'd known what I was to face!
To begin: there are years with no money
Which after so long, doesn't seem funny
A SERC mileage allowance for your car
Can you really make petrol go that far?
No occupation, no status as such
And a bank manager who says as much
You beg and ask favours from those you know
You push people, but how far will they go
Then they call you a 'lady of leisure'
Using your days as you like – what pleasure
By the end of the year, the joke wears thin
But still you hear it, day out and day in
To all of your family this is not real
But an interlude, till coming to heel
A degree was fine, career – perhaps
But do as you should and now let it lapse
You begin so convinced that this is right
But by the end it becomes such a fight
The doubts, frustration, and the silent tears
The lonely days that turn to endless years
Enthusiasm that does more than wane
And then just think – it could all be in vain!

For a Special Bear

A childhood gift so wise
You offer ageless solace
Through knowing, caring eyes
And gentle, loving face

My faithful, footboard friend
What secret fears you hide
As in fights you defend
To ever keep my side

You soak up floods of tears
And ease the endless pains
You wipe away the years
With love that never wanes

Your marmalade paws that hug
With pads time wears so fine
And arms that hold me snug
In safety to define

You hear many tantrums
Soothe ires I need to air
I know this only comes –
From such a special bear

Raindrops

The
first drop
of rain and you
proclaim. Colourful
street processions remain
in this watery domain. Jostle
for space retain. Tempt sunshine
regain. To battle in vain against the
elements gravity sustain, as water falls
and the rain stops but drips and drops and
d
r
i
p
s
a n
gai

Norfolk

Shingle beaches
Crashing wave
Pebble reaches
Search to save

Windmills turning
Tranquil peace
Power yearning
Turmoil cease

Blood red poppies
Cornfields bed
Symbolic copies
Of the dead

Floodlit spire
Cuts the night
Still stones acquire
Ageless fight

Watery veins
Broads and fen
Peaceful remains
Choked by men

Norfolk landscape
Conflicts strain
Fragile escape
Week from pain

The Meaning of Life

A number on a computer
Letters on a list
Is how I started life's long path
To prove I exist

A name on a school register
In the graded form
Stratified by ability
Classified two norm

A national insurance code
Levies what I pay
Then tax bracketed by income
Ensures there I stay

Another divorce statistic
One of any three
Credit rated, points tally scored
To make sure that's me

A market research AB2
Pigeon-holes my life
Title assigned accordingly
Woman, mistress, wife

Sex, age, status, social class
Pass or fail defined
Then coded up appropriately
Devoid of my mind

The hidden person this obscures
Matters not a jot
So long as 'nanny' can
Take the 'I' to dot

A number, or a statistic
I'm summed up as such
It's so reassuring to know
My life is worth so much!

Playing I Spy

I like the evenings at this time of year
When set against darkness, glimpses appear
As through each window, in pools of soft light
Teasing glances, of lives seeming so right

Through picture glass is the world at a glance
Others be-netted, a secretive stance
The mullioned fragments, or peeling sills
The posh, puckered blinds, and the Ashley frills

The level of income, G plan or Stag
Classics or Robbins, can easily tag
Background and class, or the social climbers
Modernist taste, or simply old-timers

The chaos in one, with toys all awry
Conveying a house full of children I spy
The piano and books of that one there
Middle-class order, perfection so square

Men staring blankly at flickering screens
Women in kitchens, stereotyped scenes
Of gleaming surfaces, everything neat
Stolen brief visions, of being complete

Echoing images of hackneyed ads.
The soap packet children, dogs, mums and dads
The retirees who live in such calm
Surrounded by photos and potted palm

Pictures that they were successful at this
All underlining, my life's gone amiss
Suburban vistas of lives they've made good
But would they change windows if they now could?

Do they like me want to move down the street?
Transform existence, seek happy retreat
For what do they see, when they walk on by
To peer deep in my world, playing I spy.

Reading Station

A station platform in the gloom
The brash announced blurring boom
Amorphous mass criss-cross their tracks
As students grasp their garish sacks

Businessmen inventing purpose
Playing out the rat race circus
Blandly, brief-cased and be-suited
Leisure, pleasure or commuted?

As others who without pretence
Just jostle bags in self-defence
Await in silence for their fate
Time redefined – early or late

As diverse reasons, never known
Are relayed on from station 'phone
Train delayed or going on time
All acted out as though in mime

Awaiting there to restart lives
Move on to loved ones, maybe wives
As solo paths converge as one
It's one chance meeting come and gone

The rich and poor, the young and old
Departures or arrivals told
By joy or pain shown on faces
To rerun scenes, times and places

Be it Reading, Kings Cross or Ware
Paddington or Leicester Square
Glimpsing fragments so alluring
Fleeting visions, yet enduring

For as the seconds tick on by
I watch and wait and wonder why
So many paths can cross again
But life is just one more missed train!

Blackpool

The tower, the funfair and Golden Mile
Illuminations stretching erstwhile
Another morning, another town
A different conference, one more frown

Isolated gatherings nationwide
Content of papers as an aside
Manchester last week, tacky surround
As Berlin the next, to feign foreign ground

With their merging of rooms all into one
The bland uniformity here has gone
As reaching out across blanket sea
Reminders of who I used once to be

The dim distant view of a life gone past
Will you survive, pleas that you'll last
Is it such arrogance here on my part
You want us to meet before you depart?

Or have I disappointed beyond all hope
Is it better I go, and leave you scope
For fond memories of that which we shared
Such private jokes, such stubbornness dared!

Whilst I've only known a third of your life
You've watched all mine, as daughter then wife
Yet so much I glimpsed through tales you retold
You brought past to present, merged young and old

The decades I'd seen in school history books
Gained proud purpose through your words and looks
As you put in context what went before
And knowing you there guaranteed more

In youthful wisdom you imparted on
To link generations, spanning so long
But I know our time's now running out
And one day too soon it won't be just doubt

Yet even now, in your unwitting way
I sense your presence, this autumn day
As at these lights, I can even smile
How you would have hated this Golden Mile!

Canterbury Cathedral

A pilgrim's focus of weary feet
The polished steps that upward meet
An inner sanctum, womb-like place
Of wood carved seats and ageless grace

In candlelight that flickers on
Sing choristers to praise in song
Amid the tombs of those long dead
And words of prayer so quietly said

Soul searching, reached through towering might
As arches aim stained rays of light
To colour hopes and fears that pass
In unified, yet private, mass

California Dreaming

With cable cars that skyward climb
And airplane lights that gently mime
Their neon way across the bay
To leave the dreams that often stay

Within this place that gave such fun
Of beaches silent in the sun
Where silly names were carved until
Pacific tides did dare to fill

With oysters eaten as a dare
As friends so distant time to share
And fortune cookies for the brave
Gave future readings just to save

As Chinatown proclaimed its fate
And sunset sank o'er Golden Gate
The San Andreas left its mark
With faultless views by light and dark

Through Stanford's hacienda-styled
Towers and arches, students smiled
Amid the tourists' Wharfside throng
Sea lions barked their farewell song

As evening cruise left 'forty-nine'
Mid panoramic scenes to dine
All 'yellow-blooded' as the rest
Again united – way out west

But then my plane joined earlier lights
Amid the east'ly leaving flights
I took the petals from the meal
To know, for once, the dream was real

Dover

Generations' warfare
Have plagued this grassy mound
As centuries of men
Have bloodshed here found
From Norman stone grey keep
To Hellfire Corner caves
The smell of death to seep
Through porous chalk-lined graves

From arrows and gunfire
To an atomic blast
This was man's aspire
To enemy outlast
As cliff-face, casemate moles
Hidden deep in ground
With God above for souls
Had killing faith profound

Today invaders pay
To see what went before
As man still kills away
But on another shore
And Dover fights unseen
New moles of Transmanche link
As ferries ply between
Now – economic brink

The Guardian

The war in Bosnia
The sad plague of AIDs
Political scandals
And IRA raids

As bombs for Oxford Street
Add to the gloom
So Somalia starves
And civil wars loom

German economy
Hits all time low
As the Highlands suffer
Cut off by snow

Indian parliament
As crisis reigns
European union
Maastricht's remains

The NHS closures
Axe Guy's and Bart's
As business falters
With few new starts

Ford workers and miners
Add to the toll
Of three million queuing
Now for the dole

What would we do, without
Quality press?
To enlighten, inform
And then depress!

Death

The stench of urine in airless heat
Workhouse surroundings – our final meet
As eyes say it all, you gasp in pain
You held on so long, for me again

Brief conversation, bridging two years
Forgiving glances, shielding the tears
As held behind glass – glimpse of delight
Four generations of yours unite

Stabbing envy, it should have been me
To give you the joy you fleetingly see
Heartfelt promises – I'd see you soon
Vain words as you died that afternoon

Whilst we all parted to go our ways
You concluded yours, leaving a–daze
'Til on Christmas Eve, in frozen cold
Reeling emotions finally took hold

The guilt, jealousy, anger and fears
The grateful relief, and then the tears
Love and compassion, you still cared such
Despite what I'd done, to give so much

Self-employment

I'm tired and frustrated, bored and broke
The only answer – go for a soak!
Find inspiration, relax alone
And get away from the bloody 'phone

I've had enough of reports and files
Tedious papers lying in piles
The legislation that makes no sense
Formatted so to make you feel dense!

Chaotic accounts that need my time
Yet seem devoid of reason or rhyme
Form a numeric war of attrition
Planned to defy simple addition

Creating a business that isn't there
And what the hell – does anyone care?
A paper to write, guidelines to draft
All for no money – I must be daft!

Articles arguing this one cause
But there's no-one there to spot the flaws
What if it's wrong, or way out of touch?
The responsible nerves dread as much

One more conference, I just can't face
Dated computer I can't replace
A car unpaid for – clocking the miles
Financial fears erasing the smiles

The ulcers, headaches, eyestrain and more
Poses the question – what's it all for?
It's better than working, that's for sure
But self-employment, is this the cure?

As tired, frustrated, bored and broke
I think I will now go for that soak
And try to ignore the bloody 'phone
Yet grateful that my time is my own!!

Neutral Ground – Matlock Bath

We share a laugh and feed the koi
In troubled waters deep
Amid the pouring rain and damp
The moist reminders seep

Our fingers now devoid of rings
So poignantly once given
A brief respite, a few snatched hours
The end of miles driven

You hand me food to cast aloft
Into the thermal spring
That at one time, long ago
Heard happy voices sing

The brooding clouds amid the cliffs
To echo our deep fears
At recreating what we had
With mutual grey tears

We've made mistakes, yet come so far
To let it slip away
But moving on amid the doubts
We both want time to stay

Brighton Pavilion

As dreaming dragons fly aloft, amid the Chinoise fake
The palm trees reach their dated height, of Cruce and Nash's make
Minarets and onion domes, in sculptured beige Bath stone
Ostentatious opulence, of overtly Regent tone

The grotesque gasoliers, with belying gentle glow
Illuminate excesses, the eye perceives below
Of fantasy and fortune, amassed with conscious care
Rotundity of rooftops, to dupe dynastic dare

An optical illusion to deceive the naked eye
Through palacette façade that feigns a foreign tie
To ensconce a regal ego that ran amok inside
A tangible repository for fiction to reside

Epsom Downs

I can almost hear you laughing
As you cast aloft my kite
I can almost see you smiling
As it falls from out of sight

I can almost feel your tension
As we watch our horse come in
And sense the shared relief
As yes – it did just win!

I can almost see your face
As we play the fairground show
And see the lights reflected
In cascading firework glow

I can almost feel your touch
As we stand and watch the planes
And almost tread your footprints
In patterned mud remains

But the visions fade from view
As I walk to where I cried
The day you once decided
Far off was your reside

To the hilltop Grandstand view
Where I grieved for Grandpa so
Bereft of the support
You said you'd always show

And to where I watched alone
The evening flights above
As you proved what was to be
Your true and lasting love

Atlanta

This brave Atlanta, brash and bold
Where Coca-Cola has the hold
Of modern faith in 90s life
Forgotten now is MK's strife

A phoenix rising from the ash
Where Sherman's army dared to smash
The Southern antebellum state
Where slaves outlived ages' fate

Stone Mountain stands aloof to bear
The testimony of the dare
Confederate against the Fed
Into the battle blindly led

With fighting lines redrawn today
Homeless blacks now wait all day
As darkened shadows stand in line
'Neath the gilded rooftop sign

For food from missions down the street
As tourists underground retreat
New class divisions now take hold
In brash Atlanta, brave and bold

The High Court

Along marble floor
Through security gaze
Turn pleading looks
Through tearful haze

Await eager postings
Along the great hall
Hear echoing footsteps
Prior judgements now fall

To wait in the pews
Amid gothic stance
The final preparing
Of one brief, last chance

Amid cloistered hush
The last tension span
Reaches its apex
And faces come wan

Flowing in black
With clergy-like frown
Be-wigged and be-suited
Each trailing gown

Take clattering files
On piggyback rides
As scarletly bound
Each case confides

Hard-hitting heels
Shoot out gunshot noise
To rattle the nerves
And re-test the poise

Called to go forward
Reporters on cue
Words at the ready
Mid green regal hue

Raised in silence
Beneath gilded crest
Sit . . . leather-bound tomes
The ultimate test

Carves nerve of steel
As accusations begin
Through veiled becalm
Now pleading to win

Watch Roman numerals
No reason or rhyme
Painfully slowly
They redefine time

As recess redraws
The battle line stance
Queen's bench division
Justice – par chance

Avid actors resume
Their teasing lead role
As tortuous silence
Just peels to the soul

The fears and the doubts
As confidence takes
Their onslaught attack
That cares not the stakes

As personal dignity
– professional views
Are mercilessly torn
As each they accuse

The final decision
Determines just lives
A cruel legal playground
Few others survive.

Moving House

Life boxed up, marked room by room
Sits in cardboard, faceless gloom
Redirect the mail that's due
Reconnect the 'phone line through

Car insurance reassessed
On-street parking? – one more test
Gas, electric, bills come in
Memories – filed in the bin

Parcelled fragments, muddled up
Treasured gifts with kitchen cup
Sentimental with the plain
Why do I have to move again?

Yet another set of fees
To acquire yet more new keys
I trade past years for future hope
This limbo transfer – can I cope?

Aching back and endless dust
Carpet cleaning – all are cussed
Wasteful time spent rearranging
Dislocation – self-estranging

TV licence, driver's too
Contents cover – changes due
Nagging panic – what's been missed?
So – make another 'must do' list!

Inventory to count me out
Rented existence – 'me' in doubt
No home, or roots – merely abode
Once again – I hit the road

Innocence Lost

The eyes of a child
So open and wide
Trusting and loving
Emotions relied
As needs are expressed
Truth is assumed
Responses assured
And kindness presumed

The eyes of a girl
Start querying looks
Realising the simple
Hides too many rucks
Through painful learning
Find nuance and tone
As lies redefine
And trusting re-hone

The eyes of a woman
Seeing death and decay
Have learnt that the words
Say not what they say
Found fears should be shown
When no one is there
Witnessed false meaning
Devoid of true care

The eyes of the wise
Wage practised pretence
Doubting and searching –
Essential defence
And know no way back
To innocence lost
We can see as a child
But know to our cost

Derby Day Evening

Police parade of cars and trucks
Winning smiles mid soulful looks
Betting slips strewn far and wide
Elated faces, mark high tide
Ice cream convoys wend their way
Hide overnight whilst others stay
To play the funfair – eat the chips
A sea awash with gypsy ships

Re-rolled turf to break the course
Only absent is a horse!
Crumpled suits, top hat and tails
Mid the brash and beery males
The nouveau riche still picnic on
Defiant islands – standing strong
As coaches set their snails' pace
Another end to one more race.

Night-time Fight

I hear the church clock strike the hour
As we bicker on
I hear the chorus mark its dawn
And question why so long?
The night-time seems
Devoid of sleep
When alone I crave
The sanctuary of book and peace
This loneliness to waive

Isle of Man Evening

The lighthouse blinks its lazy eye
Sees sea away to ponder why?
The promenade a sleepy daze
Towards the mainland fears I gaze
The thirties' airport – Biggles style
In nestling coves boats wait awhile
And whitewashed buildings centuries on
Set tranquil setting – time long gone
Clamouring cliffs 'neath seagulls' cry
Frame mirrored Mourne in sunset sky
Velvet dusk, sighs sea and sand
Then darkness turns its gentle hand
As pearly drops unclasp the night
Illuminate the seaboard sight
Extended arms of Douglas Bay
Embrace the end of peaceful day . . .

Weekend Partner

You flit in and out of my life
– though a moth
Seeking the light
– avoiding the wrath
A part-time existence
Pulling at strings
Leaving mid morning
As though you had wings

A brief fleeting presence
– elusively known
Temporary basis
– is all that is shown
A candlelight flicker
Snuffed in the breeze
Another departing
'Til next weekend's pleas

Regent's Park

The buggied brigade
Take their afternoon stroll
With dungareed kids
Making them whole
Tricycles ridden
Ducks fed and replete
Others' parenting
Scenes set complete

'Neath ice cream dribbles
Each cheeky young grin
Knows that once given
Hearts they can win
As maternal sighs
Give way to a hug
The loving exclusion
Precludes with a tug

The weekly interface
Of lives set apart
By the purpose division
That children chart
Between those who belong
To each Sunday park
And the childless souls
Who, unknowing, they mark

The Hotel Room

I look in the mirror
And see my ghost
A hollow face
In this soulless host
Another bland room
To house my shell
As memories haunt
This expensive cell
The reflected image
Cracked – decayed
I turn away
Bitter – dismayed

Paxos

This island of peace
Set in Ionian blue
Cascading olive trees
In silvery glow
Tumble down terraces
Over lichen-clad wall
As campaniles silent
Proudly stand tall
Silent – defiant
In afternoon heat
To counter the plaintive
Hobbled goats' bleat

Deserted holdings
Of Venetian calm
Netted in shady
Olive-bathed balm
The windmill of Kouros
Lost and then found
Tavernas aplenty
Ouzo's home ground
Scooters putt-putting
Their risky long climb
As boats a bob-bobbing
Their sleepy nod mime

Pittsburgh

A steel-grey city
In winter grip
Where icy rivers
So quietly slip
Beneath my window
And out to the west
While Conrail trucks
Rattle their best
The towering glass
Brash modern gleams
Pittsburgh just ain't
All that it seems!

With riverboat cruises
In paddleboat style
Another fun evening
We dance for a while
And wander the square
Where restaurants and shops
Stand where the trains
Once made their stops
Taking the inclines
Climb Washington heights
Amid the fresh snow
To watch the bright lights

Searching through Hornes
For buses and ties!
To the fountain spray
That evasion belies
Soaking the park
Where rivers merge
A fleeting focus
From which we diverge
And this marks the point
I must call it a day
Saying goodbye
And leave Pittsburgh, PA!

History

The age of elegance
In black and white
When ladies wore suits
Pinched waist tight

And men were rugged
But charming, debonair
History portrayed
In sepia square

Hotel Breakfast

The continental or the cooked
Old age glasses overlooked
Show disapproving, staring eyes
From pensioners amid the fries!
As through the napkined quiet hush
Each word receives a silent shush

I sit and watch in awed dismay
Marriages cracked, by years' decay
Such absence of contact, nothing said
Breaking the code, where looks kill dead
Do they ever talk – ever share?
Or do they yearn a youthful dare?

This start to their day, dreary, dour
Show partnerships stale and sour
Their empty vessels await their fill
Sitting, prim in their hotel drill
As their lives sound a hollow ring
Trapped behind what is the 'done thing'

Kellar

Your floppy ears
And sad, sad eyes
Your candid nose
And gaze so wise

Your practised look
Of cheeky stance
To lead me on
One merry dance

The chewed up shoes
Dismembered rug
You waddle off
With puppy shrug

One colour short
Of beagle true
But I'll take you just
The way you're you

House Hunting

Invading their privacy
I enter the door
Gasp at the decor
Can I stand more?
Patterned carpets
In garish, red shades
Blends with the curtains
Of streaked blond fades.

I open the cupboard
Her clothes hang still
Where is her family?
Just counting the will
Anxious for money
She's bundled away
Housed in a home
Or passed on her way

Photos of daughters
Watch each viewers' face
Gleaning the wealth
A macabre, grim race
With agents as reapers
In this Hades of life
Where new starts begin
With this painstaking strife

Divorce

The childhood fall with graze and cut
Peer groups from which we're cruelly shut
First love affair to blow so cold
It's then Hooke's Law begins to hold

To the maximum – undefined
Life, each time, realigned
Bouncing back as physics states
The ageing process accelerates

Elastic limit pre-assigned
Ductile or brittle personal mind
Proportionality the load
A mathematician's cosy code

For life's endless tension span
Reaching beyond where no one can
Recover the person from the mess
The ultimate, the tensile stress

Going Home

The endless grey tarmac of the motorway north
Leaving the Chilterns, I keep going forth
Past Preston bypass, awash with red cones
Hills then give way to the current day tones
As the radio tunes to the latest 'Bay' sounds
Prompting reminders of California found
Past Ashton memorial, my Lancaster days
Where music lessons are now just a haze
To the A590 where I make a left turn
The sunlight taunts as the memories burn
When this was my place, but now seems no more
Skirting the bay to the days long before
The road signs directing to events long past
Shadows of my life that forever are cast
In the panorama I silently pass
Viewed today through harsh pained glass
On past the Swan, where we danced all night
Leven Valley school comes within sight
The homes of friends appear and then fade
Bridge the pool where we walked and played
Beyond the old farmhouse – my kitten's start
I turn the last corner with sad, heavy heart
And see what was home, come into full view
I ache to revive what was once me and you
And return to the people I no longer know
And my Lakeland life, I can never let go

Christmas '94

Another round of Christmas drinks
To toast an absent friend
I wonder where you are tonight
And where all this will end

I've dressed the silent, silver tree
I wish you could but see
And wonder who you're with tonight
And what next year will be

VJ Day

Twenty tons of fireworks
That set the sky alight
Celebrate events long gone,
For you tonight
An unknown face,
A far forgotten war
Words recounting vividly
What it was you saw

A distant conflict
Arcs cast in the haze
Tainted by the sodium
A peacetime urban glaze
All so dislocated
Un-synchronised in time
As distance inculcated
Your painful wartime rhyme

Emergency Landing at Kennedy

Ten minutes to landing
Yet four hours out
Give up your trays
Stewardesses shout
A white misty sheet
Of low hugging gloom
Envelopes the feat
Of impending doom

To sink even lower
Gravity can't hide
Hitting askew, runway full tilt
Ambulances aside
Conversations wilt
In buffeting sway
We wonder how close
But no one will say

Rain dripping through
The terminal roof
Airline staff remain
Unbending, aloof
Uncertain, unknowing
We sit, stare and wait
As airline, uncaring
Decides upon fate

We reclaim baggage
From chaotic dark hulk
Jostle with carts
The cold, tired bulk
Of Flight 64
Wends its way
To wait on the sidewalk
For allotted stay

A cab to Manhattan
In the eerie dawn
The Staten Isle ferry
Departs in the morn
As New Yorkers awake
To the usual chill day
We cope with exhaustion
With us to stay

For a further journey
To where – unknown
Re-assigned, we question
And reach for the 'phone
To be woken mid morning
From three hours' sleep
Another bus ride
At Empire State peep

As we wearily pass
Once more on our way
To begin yet another
Suspended day
Amid the confusion
Re-book our flights
To cities far flung
We journey through night

To reappear briefly
In another place
The faces translate
To problems each face
By a temporary suspension
Dislocated, displaced
From loved ones expecting
And meetings replaced

NY stories revealed
Of Disney trips marred
The Girobank deal
Irretrievably scarred
An operation missed
The heart-rending start
Of dreamed of reunions
As a flight fell apart

And three hundred lives
That met up one night
As unexpected friends
With humour to fight
The fear, frustration
Exhaustion and cost
Of our finely tuned lives
When a schedule is lost

A close call that made
Each one of us think
How sad that it takes
A peer over the brink
To make us discover
The futile pace of our lives
And that only then
Such compassion survives

Adulthood

Blood is thicker than water
So the old saying goes
As we reassemble together
The faces each other knows

From photographs and stories
Retold twelve thousand miles away
By parents who are linked
In this old familial way

Our present lives fragmented
Are scattered far apart
Divided by career and children
But provide a fragile start

As past history's refocused
Yet with common threads we weave
Our own tapestry of patterns
To heal the years that cleave

And a decade on we build
Our own generation's ties
Of the family that binds
Through our independent lives

You with a husband and children
In your foreign lands
Me – a divorce behind me
Yet we feel the common strands

As women now full grown
We discover much shared ground
Renew a childish friendship
Through the adult links we've found

This inexplicable tie
Which we saw our parents share
Of unquestioning support
Is now ours, for which we care.

Key West

Banyan trees in restful pose
Beyond the Duval crawl
Of tourists' laughter ringing out
In famous Sloppy Joe's

Conch cruisers coast this gilded isle
Sedately passing time
Between the palms and whitewashed decks
As life just waits awhile

Martello towers protect their peace
In luscious hollow glades
Hemingway house, and Truman's place
Provide pleasing release

Linking the past with present fun
In this bejewelled key
As Mallory's dockside rev'llers
Honour its famous sun

For Colour

The paper today reported
On a fragment of our past
That prompted me to wonder
What happened, as the decade cast

The die that moved our lives apart
In separate spheres unknown
As we became women – independent
Of all we'd shared and known

And I think of you tonight
My long-lost friend of then
When in Jesmond Road we debated
Poetry, issues, life and men

The little tiny cat we shared
– Of Alice, Judith, Sarah, Sue
But of all the common threads
I wonder what became of you?

Who prompted initial meaning
To debates that changed our lives
Of feminism, and Greenham
The independence that survives

Of female solidarity
That beyond married days survived
And provided inspiration
Today, memories of you revived.

Unfair Legacy

Solitude so pleasant
Loneliness such pain
Laughter incandescent
Alone yet again

Fun so effervescent
A distant refrain
The desperate descent
To blackness again

So promises allure
Contrast real life
A tantalising cure
Security or strife?

Or abstract illusions
Offering ways out
But means then are lacking
Casting present doubt

Real intimations
Of a better day
Pricey implications
Are then what you say

Worthy anticipation
Of years as required
My participation
Is this love inspired?

Overt obligations
Justify your deals
Arrogant assumptions
That biding time heals

Stating, oh, so clearly
I go alone or wait
Then declaring dearly
Condoning this fate

Assured by the depth
Of my love for you
You've strength enough to say
So long or make do

Prepared now to gamble
With my life this way
Deeming future perfect
Will present tense outweigh

Yet adding more lost years
To those already missed
Holding out for years
With present so dismissed

Raises realisation
Life may pass me by
That forsaking time for you
Could leave me asking why?

I went on hoping, when
Despite the present tense
You deemed future giving
Made sufficient sense

Goodbye

I've binned your postcards
Consigned to the heap
The clothes I bought you
So dear yet so cheap

Three years of hoping
Pointless lost dreams
A series of tears
Is all it now seems

Three years of chances
Of just one more try
With my screaming heart
Saying but why?

When empty promises
Have fallen to dust
And love ceased to be
Even passable lust

So the flat echoes now
Empty and still
With places and pictures
You no longer fill

Goodbye II

Our dreams are now consigned
to the haze of the past
From your critical judgement
shadows are no longer cast
As my emotions and senses
now delight in the day
And memories of your face – fade
from black to pale grey

Thirty-somethings

I met you today – as a colleague and friend
A kindly meeting for a stress-free week's end
A white carnation as an amusing token
That prompted discussion, of issues unspoken
So many thirty-somethings, with no time for soul
Where career paths move
And whose lives take their toll

Dubai

A mystery voice with alluring tone
Entered my life as a voice on the 'phone
An airport meet, in the dusky heat
Deserted beach, with wave-lapped feet
Boundless conversing, laughter shared
Consummate questions – passions dared
In a city of mosques, where scents and sound
Create sparkling mirage – masking profound?
A desert storm, blitzing the dark night
Leaving, to question a fantasy flight?
And shed precious orchids, consign a dream
Defining Dubai, and what might have been
As Lebanese charm – again exerts its force
Touches my life – and changes its course

Playing with Words!

Miss, mistrusted, and then misled
Woman defined, by the language that's said
Misdirected, much misunderstood
Misused, mistaken, sets out womanhood

Masters, masterfully contemplate
Defining masculine – and women's fate
Masthead – sets leader, and mast the lynch pin
As mastectomy starts cutting within

Miss, the inviting, misdirect
Making a pass, and then slowly dissect
Missus, equating mythical stress
Or mistress spelling stupendous distress!

Master, the positive mastermind
Marking the mantra of man, and mankind!
Missing a negative prefix where . . .
Language creates such a mismatched affair!

As women from Venus, men from Mars
Try to establish joint lives mid the stars
Each conversing in their gender prose
No wonder the result's – only heaven knows!

Diana

A nation mourned
The public wept
You lost your life
The country kept
A silent vigil
Mid floral bouquet
To challenge aloud
The established way

A princess who was
The face of the press
Hiding a private life
In harrowing mess
That this generation
Understood as its own
And echoed it all
In unprec'ent'd tone

The pain and anguish
Divorce, and despair
Of thirty-somethings
Who still want to care
Recognised the image
As their personal fate
And called for a future
Where your princes relate

Indy Nights

With a slow, steady climb, Chicago slips from sight
Into the inky limbo, dreams again take flight
Of Indy nights, and 'yellow' days,
And Slipp'ry Noodle blues
With Stateside friends whose company I choose

The school bus hack, amid fall maples glowing gold
And theatrical roulette loses chips untold
Old Speedway cars and Brickyard meal
Election vict'ry gain
Yearly trade show chat, acquaintances regain

The Eagle's Nest revolves, its panoramic view
An eerie skyline setting, for New York adieu
To take the floor for one last dance
At Ike's, a friendly hug
Marks goodbye to Indy, and makes the heart strings tug

With sunrise over Ir' land, night abruptly ends
From Mid Atlantic mem'ries, real life descends
As past and present carousel
British customs re-bag
Collect myself, the car, and yesterday's jet lag!

Childless

Fragments of memories, passions past
Glittering fragments, moments cast
A personal history, I cannot relay
In that enigmatic parental way

Of one generation on to the next
Inscribed in familial oral text
Of mystical people that elders once were
Experience valued and then to share

A Lesson in Politics

I watch your stance, as you take to the floor
Question your lines, as you answer one more
Fleetingly passing from one to the next
Both reading a scripted, preordained text
Defined by the servants who sit out there
Who know not what, or for whom that you care

We share a brief joke, as questions defend
Enjoy the moments that all too soon end
I study you both, in silent, drawn pose
Admire your strength in the roles you chose
And pity the lines you both have to fake
As people the press too cruelly forsake

I read your papers with their party lines
Decipher scribbles the real you defines
In snatched, shared seconds, away from the glare
Find two able people trying to care
A Cabinet reshuffle rumoured loud
Yet despite the stress you still face my crowd

Leaving me asking, could I do as well
The brief, the workload, the media hell
I see your features so shadowed by stress
But understand why you face such duress
The political highs, the need to play
I'd give it a shot, and as you, would pay!

Me and my CV

With our O levels and A's
Come music and sport
The whole person reflected
In our first, brief report

As degrees can be added
We now play the game
And the social persona
Is removed from the frame

As careful, chosen phrases
Take on centre stage
Publications are added
At appropriate age

And experience is packaged
In saleable roles
No obvious omissions
Or gaping grey holes

As callously rebranded
We gain middle age
The profess'nal created
By concise, precis'd page

A clinical construction
For the world to see
Now obfuscated, hidden
The person this should be!

The Rumour Mill

So the rumour mill is turning, gaining speed
Scooping speculation with voracious greed
Fuelled on by stale phrases, all heard before
As boredom, tut-tutting, accumulates more

A no-win situation, where any contact will
Prompt more tortured turns of this seedy mill
Where denials undeserving, are cited with glib glee
But silence will be sentenced as a guilty plea

Scatter myriad emotions; prompts amazed reply
My name could be linked with this gentle guy!
And then upon reflection, a personal, wry grin,
They think we have the time for such adult'rous sin!

Once more, resignation, this prescribes my life
A female profess'nal, who isn't a wife
Is therefore on the make, a moral-less whore.
And sex is established as the ration'l more

Profound disappointment, their lives are so sad
Their only excitement, to speculate so bad!
Irate at the prospect, of the gossip's gain
The insidious remnants, too often, remain

Leaving deep lasting anger this time at stake
A trusted confidante, they've no right to take
True friendship and humour are merely person'l loss
As the rumour mill moves on – it gathers no moss!

Criminal Justice

The low slung buildings
Set in landscaped grounds
Classes in computing
Industrious sounds
Peacocks strut, strutting
In warm summer sun
Belying the purpose
For which I have come

The beige metal cell
With integral sink
Where bullies should ponder
Makes me now think
As I move to remand
With its threatening noise
I listen to officers
Their profess'nal poise

I stand dismayed
That eight hundred so young
Have moved into Feltham
The final grim rung
On a ladder of crime
From which few progress
And seek the answers
To this expensive distress

Saddened that such metal cells
With strip search routine
Are better than life
And all it should mean

On the Bench

A teasing teenager who caught your eye
Harmless flirting by a middle-aged guy
Innocuous feelings with an innocent face
That misinterpreted caused this disgrace

Or a repeated pattern of insidious form
That deviated from accepted norm
Premeditated, so carefully groomed
Silent reaction, of victim assumed

Temptation taunting, in adult repose
Dressed to kill mid flaunting flared clothes
Inviting and willing to your lonely eye
But you didn't backtrack or say goodbye

And so now you face today in the dock
Our silent court with its timeless clock
And we sit in silence deciding your fate
Agonising on, your sentence we weight

To reach our decision, searching we find
The balance of justice, the chair now defined
And with careful method our logic we check
Knowing either way it's a life that we wreck

Securicor move to stand their ground
The court hushed, our words rebound
Broken, defeated, escorted away
Three months inside is what you now pay

Protected by paper as far as we can
The warrant is signed to break this man
That society will label onward for life
Knowing it's we who wielded the knife

Aware tomorrow you could be found dead
Hanged in a cell, or alone in your bed
Politics, emotions and law we must square
Critical decisions, we daily must bear

As we leave the court with heavy heart
Our decision subjected to appellate chart
And three of us face the rest of our day
Box private emotions, and go on our way

Dancing

From one brief meal, we shared long ago
The fleeting glances, I could never let go
Through imposed separation, best for both sides
Careful reactions, with passions denied
Reacquainted over dinner, in business stance
Knowing it's starting this dangerous dance

From one stolen stay your presence remains
In erotic images the grey morning feigns
Was it an illusion, all that we shared?
The hours of passion, the emotions bared
Light laughter and touch, tousled and free
Is this really happening to you and me?

The First Snow of Winter

As the first snow of winter
Touches earth
– with its white velvet glove
I watch you wake in my bed
And for the first time
– know I've fallen in love

Scandal

The media hacks are sniffing blood
Salacious story of church no good
Libellous phrases, taunting new year
To prey on the nerves, prompting deep fear
Hideous headlines, hard, haunting ghosts
Daily potential of Morning Posts
Where Evening Standard, painful line
Defenceless waiting, now undermine

You've joined ranks with the written about
Who've read our names, and silently shout
At black on white, when shades of grey
Reflects reality but, of course, doesn't pay
The daily diets of others' pasts
That sells newspapers, but briefly casts
Dark shadows across the lives they mar
Leaving others to heal the scar

But please remember, those who know
Ignore what the papers daily show
Have also been there, and ignore snide slant
Their petty poison, vindictive rant
And for whom you're but an unknown face
It is no more than a brief, bad disgrace
Providing relief, we're all the same
Struggling, and failing, to play the game

Even those who believe what they've read
Seek only fleet comfort from words been said
And experience shows those who care
Care not what the media deign to share
And understand what you're going through
Make their own minds as to what is true
Know you'll survive, and gain from this hell
And, by empathy, not press, it'll tell!

The Beach

I pick up a stone cast on the beach
Heart-shaped perfection – but you're out of reach
I watch the light settle, on salted sand
And ache for your presence
The touch of your hand

I pick up a stone cast by the tide
Desktop reminder – of our daily divide
I watch the horizon far to the south
And ache for your presence
The taste of your mouth

I pick up a stone cast on the beach
The one fragile link – this divide can breach
I watch the sun's shadow, wanting you there
And ache for your presence
Here now and to share

Moving On

I can go no further with this cause or rite
No longer have the will to stay and fight
I need a few months to ponder, reflect
Determine my future, and past dissect

To rescue my body, my soul and my mind
And a purpose regain, re-establish, re-find
Devoid of the worry, the anguish, the pain
Step back from the fast track, where seasons remain

To wake in the morning refreshed and alert
Seeking the day, with challenge not hurt
Not bitter and broken, but hopeful and sure
Where faith is renewed, and ready for more

In Fifteen Years of Adulthood –

I've danced to fourteen nations' beat
And travelled miles long haul
Used up at least some thirteen lives!
Employed twelve staff in all

Spent eleven years in studious 'fun'
Lived in homes that number ten
Nine years donated to voluntary cause
'Longside eight of business won

I've shared seven years of marriage.
Of Beaglehood I've six
Eamed five worthy publications
With four degrees to mix

Three lifelong friends have seen me through
From true love to heartbreak – twice
And just one bitter sweet regret
To mark fifteen years of spice!